Booga Bear Publishing

ALSO BY MARY B. MORRISON

JUSTICE JUST US JUST ME

SOUL MATES DISSIPATE

MARY B. MORRISON

Who's
Making
Love

Always make love, especially during sex.

PUBLISHED BY
Booga Bear Poetry Group Publishing
P. O. Box 23027
Washington, DC 20026

Library of Congress Control Number: 2001129021

ISBN 0-9674001-7-1

Printed in the United States of America

May 2001

First Printing

10 9 8 7 6 5 4 3 2 1

Editor: Hettie Jones

Jacket Design by: The Image House

Photograph by: Tarik Jones

Dedicated to my son
Jesse Bernard Byrd, Jr.

Thanks

I thank God for my countless talents, including my ability to write in several genres. I'm grateful the Lord has blessed me with a wonderful son, Jesse Bernard Byrd, Jr. In addition, I don't know what I'd do if I didn't have the love and support of my siblings, Wayne, Derrick, Andrea, and Regina Morrison, Margie Rickerson, and Debra Noel. I'm thankful for the infinite wisdom my father —Joseph Henry Morrison— shared with each of us. His knowledge has allowed me to breathe life into his spiritual existence. Last but farthest from least, I thank God for my mother, Elester Noel. Mama, may your soul rest in peace, always.

Unconditional

Mama if I had one wish
it would truly be
to love someone other than my child
Unconditionally

I watched you, Mama
day after day
caring for the family

I saw you, Mother
time and time again
sacrificing your needs

But not just for us
for strangers too
and people you barely knew

Mama, if I had *one* wish
it would truly be
to love someone other than myself
Unconditionally

Heaven is no longer
missing its angel
but Mama I'm missing you
tell Daddy I said hello
and one day I'll see you two

Often I've said
if I had to do it all over again
I'd do it all over again
and I wouldn't change a thing

But now that you're gone
I can clearly see
If—No—When
I learn to love others unconditionally

Only then will I be free

Oh, Mama if I had *just* one wish
it would truly be
to love someone other
another and another
a sister and a brother
a spouse and a friend
and my soulmate

Unconditionally

Don't wait until tomorrow to start living for today. It's never too late. Anytime is a good time to find your ideal mate. And when you find him or her, love—*unconditionally*.

CONTENTS

INTRODUCTION

Investing in this guide could yield you the ideal relationship you've been yearning for. Keep this question in mind as you read through your self-help guide. *What kind of relationship would you like to have?* Notice that you were not asked what type of mate you would like to meet. When you shop for a car, you should know what type you want (e.g., Lexus ES300, gold metallic exterior, beige leather interior, twelve disc CD changer, etc.). However, if you're seeking to establish a meaningful relationship, you must build from the inside out. You have to start by asking yourself very pointed questions. Like "How well do I know myself?" Then you must answer truthfully.

This guide will become your keepsake memoir. Everyone won't have to journey through ten prospects to find the right person. Others may have to buy another copy of this guide and move on to number eleven and so forth. Either way, keep in mind that your objective is to find Mr. or Ms. Right. Not Mr. or Ms. Perfect.

Some of you may ask, "What makes Mary B. Morrison an expert on relationships?" I'm proud to tell you that I've graduated with honors and earned my degree in *Common Sense*. All the money in the world cannot buy good judgment. To this day, I can honestly say, "I'm friends with *every* man I've ever dated." You can't run away from your past, so you may as well make each day as pleasant as possible. Relationships are about building friendships from the very beginning. Using this guide will help you to find *your* ideal mate.

As you begin to encounter new associates, know this: there are no victims in relationships because you always have a choice. You can stay or leave; but if you decide to stay, make a commitment to make your union work. Otherwise, what's the point? Realize that men are not dogs and women aren't leeches. If you want a dog or a leech, go to the pet store and buy one, don't date one.

Throughout your quest for love, remember to always compromise but never settle. When you compromise, you mutually agree to sacrifice something in order to improve your relationship. However, when you settle, you give up something important to you hoping that it will please the other person. As a result, a part of your spirit dies, and gradually the other person will become increasingly demanding and excessively controlling. Eventually you'll become unhappy with yourself because you're no longer the person you used to be. Before you realize it, one petal at a time will have been plucked from your blossoming rose and you'll be left standing alone—a wilted stem. You are the one and only person whom you *can* control; so don't ever do this to yourself.

Learn to unconditionally love yourself first. When you love yourself, you're genuinely capable of loving anyone else. If you don't love yourself, you won't be able to love anybody else. Sure you can trick yourself into believing that you can. But deep down inside, if you don't love yourself you won't be able to sustain a healthy relationship. There's a difference between more and first. It's all right to place someone else's needs before your own. If you have children, you probably sacrifice selflessly all the time. People who love themselves will not allow others to abuse them mentally, physically, emotionally, spiritually, or otherwise. If you truly love yourself, you *will* walk away from unhealthy relationships knowing —not wondering— that you've made the right choice.

You need to document information about the prospects you meet for several reasons, and that's where this guide becomes your barometer. Sometimes you forget, suppress, and even ignore how some individuals have treated you in the past. Subconsciously you begin to attract people with similar traits. Before you know it you're right back where you started, searching for someone new (or not so new when you think about it). That's why writing down the facts is so significant.

Occasionally, you may tend to overlook essential dates, or forget the names of the other person's children, and then you may be embarrassed to ask for such noteworthy information again. More importantly, as you begin to meet more people, you will be able to determine where you're placing the emphasis in your selection criteria. You must openly and honestly evaluate this data because that will reveal why you're drawn to individuals with comparable traits.

Trust me on this one. Don't focus primarily on the physical. Too many people miss the opportunity of a lifetime to share happiness because they're too intent on the external (i.e., attractiveness, material possessions, etc.). True beauty resonates from within. Keep your trophies on the shelf and your loved one by your side.

Another factor is that women of all races —on the average— are more likely to date within their race. The exact opposite is true of men. Generally, men love women irrespective of nationality, income, or social status. Basically a man doesn't care if a woman earns five dollars a day or one hundred and fifty dollars an hour. Most women do consider the earnings of a potential mate prior to establishing a relationship. You might get lucky and find your type. But don't build your relationship based on luck because at some point your luck will run out. Besides, types are readily replaceable. If you wreck that Lexus, hey, you can go out and purchase another one. Better yet, the insurance company will foot the bill. Bodily injury and property damage are no substitutes for heartaches. Stop shopping for types and start building wholesome relationships.

Don't forget that "*Once upon a time*" always starts a fairytale. Sure there was a time when a man brought home the bacon and a woman cooked it for the family. But times have changed drastically. There are a lot of women earning higher salaries than men. The bottom line is, don't limit yourself. Every time you impose a tangible or concrete criterion for a relationship you eliminate millions of eligible mates, especially if you exclude an entire race. So if your mate has to possess a car, a house, a good job, have no kids, and be of a particular race, all I can say to you is you'll need that luck you read about earlier. You've just rejected millions of individuals who are seeking and fully capable of establishing a healthy relationship.

As far as material items are concerned, I have three words for you: get your own. Remember the *Golden Rule*. He who has the gold, rules. Nobody was put on this earth to labor for your gratification. It's nice if they decide to share, but if it was their car and house when you met them, it's exactly that— theirs. Having your own builds self-esteem. It's better to meet someone and work towards common goals. It's a crime to set your eyes on another person's possessions and then steal them away. Don't do this and don't allow this to happen to you.

From this moment forward it's essential for you to use the words *I will* or *I won't* or *I may* or *I may not*. Do not use the word *can't*. You can achieve anything you believe. You can find Mr. or Ms. Right because your ideal mate is eagerly waiting to meet you too. You don't have to conduct an hour-long interview. You have ninety days to collect and review the required information listed in Section Four. This is the minimum time that you should use to evaluate whether or not you're interested in cultivating a meaningful relationship. Be patient. Through regular conversations you will get answers to the questions.

Don't rush into a commitment or sex unless you're sure this is the person for you, especially if your goal is to get married. There is such a thing as love at first sight. But remember this: love don't love anybody. People love people. If you follow this guide, you'll have a better chance of finding a compatible companion. At the very least, you should discover why you haven't.

This guide consists of four sections. First, you're provided with the necessary information to understand each component. Next, you're given food for thought on broadening your perspective. Then, you will complete a self-evaluation that will help you better understand whether you're honestly seeking the relationship you desire. Finally, you will outline significant data that will allow you to hone in on your ideal mate.

Embrace and enjoy every step of the process. Each evaluation, with the exception of the self-evaluation, will take a minimum of ninety days. Actually, this time frame is perfect because most individuals will have taken off their mask by the time you're ready to tally up your scores. What you see in the beginning is seldom what you get in the end, but within the first three months you usually experience strong indicators signaling the relationship should not be pursued. Most people ignore these signs, hoping the person will change. Two, three, even four years later they find themselves complaining about the same things they ignored within the first three months. But thanks to this guide, you don't have to end up being one of those persons.

It's best to clearly communicate whether you're interested in establishing a relationship. Start with a smile. Always give your potential mate a compliment. Everyone enjoys having his or her ego stroked. Now, take a deep breath. Release. And get ready to find the person *your* heart desires.

Section One

This section is an explanation of how to complete the information in Sections Three and Four. You should refer back to this section as often as necessary in order to respond to each item. Because each person is unique and possess multiple desirable qualities, you'll independently develop and determine your criteria. By evaluating yourself first, you'll discover not only what kind of person you are, but also what kind of relationship you desire.

Explanation of Your Basic Information

Do not write in this section. Adequate spaces for documentation are reserved beginning on page fourteen. Listed below is the basic information you'll need to understand about yourself:

- **Name** (first, middle, last)
  There's no need to label your book on the outside. This is simply your space for identification.

- **Career**
  It's important to list the type of work you do. Take time to think about whether you honestly like your job, or if it is simply your sole provider of food, clothing, shelter, etc. Generally, people who love their career have a greater appreciation for their mate's profession. Your outlook on your career directly impacts on your relationship.

- **Hobbies**
  List the things you enjoy doing immensely just for fun.
  Everyone needs *at least* one hobby. When you have
  interests outside your relationship, you're less
  demanding of the other person's time and respectful
  when your mate wants to invest leisure time outside the
  relationship. Both parties must have mutual respect for
  one another's hobbies.

- **Favorite Colors**
  This is self-explanatory. As simple as it may seem,
  take it to the next level and analyze why you and your
  potential mate prefer these colors. Favorite colors are
  reflective of the inner spirit. Are you generally happy
  so you gravitate towards bright colors? Are you a
  strong introvert so you typically don't even notice the
  colors around you? Or are you dominating so you
  prefer bold colors? Think about the colors you and
  your mate like best.

- **Favorite Foods**
  Your palate is keen. If you love sweets, you'll take
  note immediately if that first kiss tastes like chocolate
  or lemon-lime.

- **Favorite Movies**
  Here's another introspective look at your personality.
  If you appreciate a good mystery or thriller, you may
  find an aloof and nonchalant mate very boring.

- **Favorite Activities**
Your favorite activities differ slightly from your hobbies because these are the ideal moments to include your mate. Maybe you enjoy exercising, dancing, or simply cuddling in front a nice warm fireplace listening to your favorite CD. This is where you'll be able to welcome your loved one into your world. As a result of sharing, you'll grow closer together.

- **Favorite Sports**
This includes participating and watching. If you have an appreciation for both, a mate who thinks sports are dumb is probably not the one for you. It's unhealthy to have ongoing debates regarding whether or not you should enjoy sports.

- **Parents**
List your parents and/or guardians here. Think about how you would respond to the items above if you were answering for them. Have their views affected the way you see yourself and others? Were you encouraged to express yourself openly? If not, be cautious because you may gravitate towards a mate that is exactly like your parents instead of finding one ideal for you. That is why you sometimes believe you know exactly what you want and don't understand why you keep finding mates with characteristics resembling those of your parents. Or *you* end up unconsciously mimicking your mother and father's traits.

- **Siblings**
  List your siblings. How do they impact on your decision for a mate? Often other people think they know what's best for you when they don't understand their own desires. Dismiss the expectations of your family and friends when it comes to selecting your mate. You only have one life to live. Don't waste it living up to someone else's expectations. You'll be happier.

- **Closest Friends**
  Friends are typically for forever. Relationships usually aren't. Why? Because sometimes your friends give you all the advice they would never accept from anyone else, including you. Don't wear your pride on your shoulders when it comes to the love of your life. Carry it in your heart. If you're going to end up heartbroken, do it because the relationship wasn't working well for you. Your friends will be around for your next relationship too.

- **Sex and Love**
  How often do you like to have sex and make love? The difference between the two is simpler than you may imagine. Sex is a physical act and love is an emotion. Make love to your mate every day, especially during sex. Consider whether you desire to have sex once, twice, seven days a week, or after marriage. This is important when choosing a mate. Never take love for granted. Always show your mate how much you care.

- **Baggage**
  Never compare a new acquaintance with a former mate or to the next date. This is self-defeating and interferes with your success in finding the right person. Everyone has issues. It's how you deal with your predicaments that makes the difference between establishing a healthy or unhealthy relationship. Remember each person's problems are equally valid. If you've been emotionally hurt, that's good. That means hopefully you've allowed yourself to fall in love. Everybody plays the fool sometimes. Just don't remain one. If you're waiting for Mr. or Ms. Right to be perfect, then you'll have to do just that—wait. If you're guilty of clinging to your baggage, write it down, pack it up, and send it on a one-way trip with no return to Timbuktu. Then make a conscious decision to allow each individual to stand alone on his or her merits.

- **What kind of relationship do you want?**
  Remember you were asked at the very beginning of this book to think about this question? Soon it will be time to answer. Truthfully.

- **Insert a favorite photo**
  When you look at this photo of yourself or your prospective mate, first look beyond the physical and think about how the picture makes you feel. Then look at the person and see what you adore. Write it down and refer to this page periodically over the next ninety days.

Explanation of Basic Relationship Information

Here is some basic information important to know about the individual(s) with whom you're interested in establishing a relationship. There are only four items listed here that differ from the basic information requested about yourself. Use the same criteria for items that are the same and apply them to the other person. Listed below are the new items:

- **Address (physical)**
  Always know where the person lives if you're going to date. Make certain someone close to you also knows the address.

- **Telephone numbers (home, cellular, business, etc.)**
  A potential mate should not be reluctant to provide this basic information. Reserve business numbers for urgent matters or find out when it's appropriate to call. Never disrespect anyone's place of employment.

- **Date of Birth (month, date, year)**
  This is an important date to remember.

- **Children's Names (first, middle, last)**
  Most parents love their children unconditionally. If your intent is to establish a relationship, remembering children by name is a great place to start and score points with the other person.

Explanation of the Ten Points Checklist

The information requested here is exactly the same for you and your prospects. After the explanation of the last point, there's an explanation of the scoring and rating system on page ten. Listed below are the ten points:

1. **Characteristics/Personality**
   You should know what distinctive characteristics and general disposition you would like in a mate. Always remain open-minded. However, if you know that loud and obnoxious individuals are vexing to you, don't overlook this factor when dating. The same applies to their mannerisms and overall disposition.

2. **Loyalty**
   Good mates are faithful and will stand by your side through good times and challenging moments. He or she is empathetic, supportive, and understanding. This doesn't mean the person has to agree with everything you believe and this definitely doesn't mean either of you is infallible.

3. **Trustworthiness**
   People are basically good-natured but they're not perfect. You should gravitate towards someone you can rely on. If he or she claims to be going out with the guys or girls, you shouldn't question the individual's honesty unless you have all the facts and discover otherwise. Give the person the benefit of the doubt. Think innocent until proven guilty. There's a huge difference between being insecure and having a lack of trust.

4. **Sense of Humor**

If you learn to laugh with your mate, you'll also teach yourself not to take comments personally. Appreciate the little things in life. Laughter is still the best medicine on the market. Just remember to laugh with —not at— your mate. If you find yourself laughing at your mate behind his or her back, this isn't the person for you.

5. **Things in Common**

Every couple should have several things in common. It's true that opposites attract. But exact opposites generally aren't a good match. Commonality is a catalyst for creating a successful relationship. For your self-evaluation, list things you've had in common with previous mates.

6. **Likes**

Be aware of the qualities you like about your mate and yourself. Maybe you like that he's punctual or she's considerate of your desires. The way he smiles. How she straightens your tie or the manner in which you touch your mate affectionately without saying a word.

7. **Dislikes**

We could be diplomatic here and state "Improvement Areas." But let's face the facts. Honesty is required to build healthy relationships. Dislikes are associated with varying degrees of tolerance. How strongly do feel about a person who smokes or someone who constantly interrupts you when you're speaking? Do you like arrogant people who are also inconsiderate? If there's something you don't like about your potential mate, tell him or her. Don't criticize. People are unaware of your dislikes until you reveal them.

8. **Spirituality**
   This is the ability to see and feel things that are intangible. The depth of the third eye is vital. Every source of energy in the universe is connected. If your faith is within a specific denomination, you'll need to consider the beliefs of your mate and how any differences will impact on your relationship.

9. **Family Values**
   Understanding why and how an individual values relationships with family members is critically significant. If you love your family and your mate ostracizes his or her family, this may present a challenge in maintaining your relationship.

10. **Goals**
    When completing the self-evaluation, list personal goals here. List both relationship and individual goals. Each objective should be realistic to achieve. Reserve your ultimate ambitions for your dreams. Everyone should be a dreamer with goals.

Scoring and Rating

At the end of ninety days, review the data you've recorded and document your scores. Ten is the maximum score allowed for each point on the checklist. The higher your score the greater your connection. The highest overall score possible is one hundred.

Rating Scale:
- 100-93   ideal relationship to pursue
- 92-85   very good relationship to pursue
- 84-77   healthy relationship to pursue
- 76-70   not a healthy relationship to pursue
- 69-0   don't do it

If the score is between ninety-three and one hundred, this is an ideal relationship for you, one that you should have few, if any, doubts about pursuing. Remember, nobody is perfect so it's acceptable to have concerns.

If the score is between eighty-five and ninety-two, this is a relationship worth pursuing. It's likely that you'll be able to successfully cultivate your ideal relationship within a few additional months.

If the score is between seventy-seven and eighty-four, this is a healthy relationship and you're off to a good start. It'll take time to achieve your ideal relationship, but with dedication and commitment from both partners, it can be accomplished.

A score between seventy and seventy-six indicates an unhealthy relationship that really should not be pursued. If you decide to take this chance, make a mutual commitment up front to make it better. Good luck.

Hey, let's face it. If the score is sixty-nine or below, that's probably all you'll get—*sixty-nine (as it relates to sexual intercourse) or less.*

Before long it will be time for you to evaluate and score yourself. If you don't know what you yourself want, you will not be able to evaluate your mate effectively. Section Three is all about you. This is the time to be brutally honest about the kind of person you are and the relationship you would like to have. If you cannot be truthful with yourself, don't bother to complete Section Three or any other part of this guide. You'll just be wasting your time. Most people want to be honest. If it takes you some time to think about the true answers, allow yourself that time. Then complete your list. It's okay. You shouldn't rush or force yourself to write down your responses. It should be a natural process. Once you've completed your analysis, you'll be ready to start evaluating your potential mates.

Section Two

Life Is What You Make It

There are three basic aspects to dating. One, never assume anything. Two, if you could date yourself, would you be the happiest person in the world? And three, always compromise but never settle. If you can learn to master these areas, you'll discover how easy it is to get a date and find your ideal mate.

Unless you're telepathic, don't try to read someone else's mind. If the person of your dreams asks you out on a date, don't take for granted that you're the only person he/she is dating. The rule of thumb is that almost everyone you'll meet is involved in a relationship with someone other than yourself. Learn to communicate in the affirmative. Ask questions. How many people are you dating? How many individuals are you sexually intimate with? Clearly these are two different questions that typically yield two different responses, especially from men. The bottom line is that you are only in control of yourself. Be open-minded and optimistic because positive energy sends good vibes to your potential mate.

There was a time when you couldn't meet someone unless you physically made yourself available. Now, thanks to the Internet, you don't even have to leave your home to make a new acquaintance. You have no excuse for not finding a mate. Be creative. Although I'm in a healthy relationship, here's an example of what I've done: My personalize license plate is one of my AOL screen names. The license plate guard underneath my tag reads @aol.com. Have I met anyone because of this? Absolutely. I've met several people, both males and females. Choose whatever works for you. Everyone is not as bold, so do what makes you comfortable.

Speaking of comfort, would you date yourself if you could? This is important. Most individuals search outside themselves for the relationship that will make them complete. Overall, if you're happy with yourself, mates will be drawn to you. On the other hand, if you nag or complain frequently, even inside your own head, then you've got some work to do. If you desire happiness in your relationship, you must first be happy with yourself.

In order to establish longevity with your mate, learn to compromise and be considerate. Compromise is the foundation of everything in life. Whether with your parents, your boss, your teachers, or your mate, you must give in order to receive. While you are more blessed when you give, don't sacrifice to the extent that you're not receiving anything in return.

Remember: life is never what you want it to be. Life is what *you* make it. Accept responsibility for your actions. Ask questions and don't take someone's reply to your question personally. Until you meet your ideal mate, diversify the investment of your time. Steer clear of becoming an interviewer and a reporter. Too many questions too soon can be a turn-off. And telling everything you know about your potential mate to your friends may sabotage your relationship. Take your time. Don't assume you've met that special someone after the first date because, if less than three months time has passed, you haven't been introduced to the real person.

Section Three

This section is designed for you to evaluate yourself. The explanation for each item is under Section One. Remember that you are the one person with whom you should be honest one hundred percent of the time. Examples are not provided because you must formulate your ideas. Release the creative and unique person inside you. Before you can ask for what you want, you must understand who you are.

Under *Your Ten Points Checklist*, you will score yourself. Imagine someone else determining your qualities. Often we're too quick to condemn others and reluctant to judge ourselves. Always evaluate yourself harder than others. For example, you may find it acceptable to stand someone up on a date and consider it unacceptable if this happens to you. Before you express disapproval of someone, try putting yourself in his or her shoes. This process will help you to score the people you meet objectively. Remember to laugh and smile. Life isn't that serious and most relationships are uncomplicated and easy to maintain.

Your Basic Information

Name

_____

(First   Middle   Last)

Career

_____

_____

_____

Hobbies

_____

_____

_____

Favorite Colors

_____

_____

_____

Favorite Foods

_____

_____

_____

Favorite Movies

_____

_____

_____

Favorite Activities

_____

_____

_____

Favorite Sports

_____

_____

_____

Parents' Names

_____
(Father)
_____
(Mother)
_____
(Stepfather or Guardian)
_____
(Stepmother or Guardian)

Siblings

_____

_____

_____

_____

_____

Closest Friends

_____

_____

_____

Sex and Love

_____

_____

_____

_____

_____

_____

Baggage

_____

_____

_____

_____

_____

_____

What kind of relationship do you want?

_____

_____

_____

_____

_____

_____

_____

_____

_____

_____

_____

_____

_____

Insert a favorite photo of yourself in the space below.

What makes this photo special?

_____

_____

_____

Your Ten Points Checklist

1. Characteristics/Personality

_____

_____

_____

_____

_____

_____
(Score)

2. Loyalty

_____

_____

_____

_____

_____

_____
(Score)

3. Trustworthiness

_____

_____

_____

_____

_____

_____
(Score)

4. Sense of Humor

_____

_____

_____

_____

_____

_____
(Score)

5. Things You Commonly Like

_____

_____

_____

_____

_____

_____
(Score)

6. Likes

_____

_____

_____

_____

_____

_____
(Score)

7. Dislikes

_____

_____

_____

_____

_____

_____

(Score)

8. Spirituality

_____

_____

_____

_____

_____

_____

(Score)

9. Family Values

_____

_____

_____

_____

_____

_____
(Score)

10. Goals

_____

_____

_____

_____

_____

_____
(Score)

Your Overall Score

_____/_____
Score   Date

Your Overall Summary

_____

_____

_____

_____

_____

_____

_____

_____

_____

_____

_____

_____

_____

_____

_____

Section Four

This is the section in which you'll record information obtained from the prospects you're interested in getting to know better. Don't be too quick to determine your level of interest. Take your time and pay close attention to what is being verbalized and communicated through other forms (body language, silence, changes in speech patterns, etc.).

On the ninetieth day (not before), assess each element on the ten points checklist and assign a score. There is a space provided at the beginning of each relationship for you to record the initial date you met and another space at the end to record the date you'll complete your rating. Total up your points and see where this person's overall score falls on the rating chart listed on page ten.

Depending on your personality and level of comfort, you may be able to evaluate more than one mate at a time. It's completely up to you. Life is all about having options and making the best decisions you can.

Relationship #1 Basic Information

Name

_____/_____

(First   Middle   Last   / the date you met)

Address

_____

(Street)

_____

(City and State)

_____

(Zip Code)

Telephone Numbers

_____

(Home)

_____

(Cellular/Pager)

_____

(Work)

Email

_____

(Email Address)

_____

(Website)

Date of Birth

_____

(Month/Date/Year)

Children's Names/Ages

(First	Middle	Last	Age)
(First	Middle	Last	Age)
(First	Middle	Last	Age)
(First	Middle	Last	Age)

Career

_____

_____

_____

Hobbies

_____

_____

_____

Favorite Colors

_____

_____

_____

Favorite Foods

_____

_____

_____

Favorite Movies

_____

_____

_____

Favorite Activities

_____

_____

_____

Favorite Sports

_____

_____

_____

Parents' Names

_____
(Father)

_____
(Mother)

_____
(Stepfather or Guardian)

_____
(Stepmother or Guardian)

Siblings

_____

_____

_____

_____

Sex and Love

_____

_____

_____

_____

_____

Baggage

_____

_____

_____

_____

_____

What kind of relationship does this person want?

_____

_____

_____

_____

_____

_____

_____

_____

_____

_____

_____

_____

_____

_____

Insert a favorite photo of this person in the space below.

What makes this photo special?

_____

_____

_____

Relationship #1 Ten Points Checklist

1. Characteristics/Personality

_____

_____

_____

_____

_____

(Score)

2. Loyalty

_____

_____

_____

_____

_____

(Score)

3. Trustworthiness

_____

_____

_____

_____

_____

_____
(Score)

4. Sense of Humor

_____

_____

_____

_____

_____

_____
(Score)

5. Things in Common

_____

_____

_____

_____

_____

_____
(Score)

6. Likes

_____

_____

_____

_____

_____

_____
(Score)

7. Dislikes

_____

_____

_____

_____

_____

_____
(Score)

8. Spirituality

_____

_____

_____

_____

_____

_____
(Score)

9. Family Values

_____

_____

_____

_____

_____

_____

(Score)

10. Goals

_____

_____

_____

_____

_____

_____

(Score)

Overall Score for Relationship #1

_____/_____
Score   Date

Overall Summary for Relationship #1

_____

_____

_____

_____

_____

_____

_____

_____

_____

_____

_____

_____

_____

_____

Relationship #2 Basic Information

Name

_____/_____
(First   Middle   Last   / the date you met)

Address

_____
(Street)

_____
(City and State)

_____
(Zip Code)

Telephone Numbers

_____
(Home)

_____
(Cellular/Pager)

_____
(Work)

Email

_____
(Email Address)

_____
(Website)

Date of Birth

_____

(Month/Date/Year)

Children's Names/Ages

_____

(First   Middle   Last   Age)

_____

(First   Middle   Last   Age)

_____

(First   Middle   Last   Age)

_____

(First   Middle   Last   Age)

Career

_____

_____

_____

Hobbies

_____

_____

_____

Favorite Colors

_____

_____

_____

Favorite Foods

_____

_____

_____

Favorite Movies

_____

_____

_____

Favorite Activities

_____

_____

_____

Favorite Sports

_____

_____

_____

Parents' Names

_____
(Father)
_____
(Mother)
_____
(Stepfather or Guardian)
_____
(Stepmother or Guardian)

Siblings

_____

_____

_____

_____

_____

Sex and Love

_____

_____

_____

_____

_____

_____

Baggage

_____

_____

_____

_____

_____

_____

What kind of relationship does this person want?

_____

_____

_____

_____

_____

_____

_____

_____

_____

_____

_____

_____

_____

_____

_____

_____

Insert a favorite photo of this person in the space below.

What makes this photo special?

_____

_____

_____

Relationship #2 Ten Points Checklist

1. Characteristics/Personality

_____

_____

_____

_____

_____

_____
(Score)

2. Loyalty

_____

_____

_____

_____

_____

_____
(Score)

3. Trustworthiness

_____

_____

_____

_____

_____

_____
(Score)

4. Sense of Humor

_____

_____

_____

_____

_____

_____
(Score)

5. Things in Common

_____

_____

_____

_____

_____

_____
(Score)

6. Likes

_____

_____

_____

_____

_____

_____
(Score)

7. Dislikes

_____

_____

_____

_____

_____

_____
(Score)

8. Spirituality

_____

_____

_____

_____

_____

_____
(Score)

9. Family Values

_____

_____

_____

_____

_____

_____
(Score)

10. Goals

_____

_____

_____

_____

_____

_____
(Score)

Overall Score for Relationship #2

_____/_____
   Score   Date

Overall Summary for Relationship #2

_____

_____

_____

_____

_____

_____

_____

_____

_____

_____

_____

Relationship #3 Basic Information

Name

_____/_____

(First   Middle   Last   / the date you met)

Address

_____

(Street)

_____

(City and State)

_____

(Zip Code)

Telephone Numbers

_____

(Home)

_____

(Cellular/Pager)

_____

(Work)

Email

_____

(Email Address)

_____

(Website)

Date of Birth

_____

(Month/Date/Year)

Children's Names/Ages

(First	Middle	Last	Age)
(First	Middle	Last	Age)
(First	Middle	Last	Age)
(First	Middle	Last	Age)

Career

_____

_____

_____

Hobbies

_____

_____

_____

Favorite Colors

_____

_____

_____

Favorite Foods

_____

_____

_____

Favorite Movies

_____

_____

_____

Favorite Activities

_____

_____

_____

Favorite Sports

_____

_____

_____

Parents' Names

_____
(Father)

_____
(Mother)

_____
(Stepfather or Guardian)

_____
(Stepmother or Guardian)

Siblings

_____

_____

_____

_____

_____

Sex and Love

_____

_____

_____

_____

_____

_____

Baggage

_____

_____

_____

_____

_____

What kind of relationship does this person want?

_____

_____

_____

_____

_____

_____

_____

_____

_____

_____

_____

_____

_____

Insert a favorite photo of this person in the space below.

What makes this photo special?

Relationship #3 Ten Points Checklist

1. Characteristics/Personality

_____

_____

_____

_____

_____

(Score)

2. Loyalty

_____

_____

_____

_____

_____

_____
(Score)

3. Trustworthiness

_____

_____

_____

_____

_____

_____
(Score)

4. Sense of Humor

_____

_____

_____

_____

_____

_____
(Score)

5. Things in Common

_____

_____

_____

_____

_____

_____
(Score)

6. Likes

_____

_____

_____

_____

_____

_____
(Score)

7. Dislikes

_____

_____

_____

_____

_____

_____
(Score)

8. Spirituality

_____

_____

_____

_____

_____

_____
(Score)

9. Family Values

_____

_____

_____

_____

_____

_____
(Score)

10. Goals

_____

_____

_____

_____

_____

_____
(Score)

Overall Score for Relationship #3

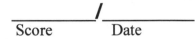

_____/_____
Score   Date

Overall Summary for Relationship #3

_____

_____

_____

_____

_____

_____

_____

_____

_____

_____

_____

_____

_____

Relationship #4 Basic Information

Name

_____/_____
(First   Middle   Last   / the date you met)

Address

_____
(Street)

_____
(City and State)

_____
(Zip Code)

Telephone Numbers

_____
(Home)

_____
(Cellular/Pager)

_____
(Work)

Email

_____
(Email Address)

_____
(Website)

Date of Birth

_____

(Month/Date/Year)

Children's Names/Ages

(First	Middle	Last	Age)
(First	Middle	Last	Age)
(First	Middle	Last	Age)
(First	Middle	Last	Age)

Career

_____

_____

_____

Hobbies

_____

_____

_____

Favorite Colors

_____

_____

_____

Favorite Foods

_____

_____

_____

Favorite Movies

_____

_____

_____

Favorite Activities

_____

_____

_____

Favorite Sports

_____

_____

_____

Parents' Names

_____
(Father)

_____
(Mother)

_____
(Stepfather or Guardian)

_____
(Stepmother or Guardian)

Siblings

_____

_____

_____

_____

_____

Sex and Love

_____

_____

_____

_____

_____

_____

Baggage

_____

_____

_____

_____

_____

_____

What kind of relationship does this person want?

_____

_____

_____

_____

_____

_____

_____

_____

_____

_____

_____

_____

_____

Insert a favorite photo of this person in the space below.

What makes this photo special?

_____

_____

_____

Relationship #4 Ten Points Checklist

1. Characteristics/Personality

_____

_____

_____

_____

_____

_____

(Score)

2. Loyalty

_____

_____

_____

_____

_____

_____

(Score)

3. Trustworthiness

_____

_____

_____

_____

_____

_____
(Score)

4. Sense of Humor

_____

_____

_____

_____

_____

_____
(Score)

5. Things in Common

_____

_____

_____

_____

_____

_____
(Score)

6. Likes

_____

_____

_____

_____

_____
(Score)

7. Dislikes

_____

_____

_____

_____

_____

_____
(Score)

8. Spirituality

_____

_____

_____

_____

_____

_____
(Score)

9. Family Values

_____

_____

_____

_____

_____

_____
(Score)

10. Goals

_____

_____

_____

_____

_____

_____
(Score)

Overall Score for Relationship #4

_____/_____
Score   Date

Overall Summary for Relationship #4

_____

_____

_____

_____

_____

_____

_____

_____

_____

_____

_____

_____

Relationship #5 Basic Information

Name

_____/_____
(First   Middle   Last   / the date you met)

Address

_____
(Street)

_____
(City and State)

_____
(Zip Code)

Telephone Numbers

_____
(Home)

_____
(Cellular/Pager)

_____
(Work)

Email

_____
(Email Address)

_____
(Website)

Date of Birth

_____

(Month/Date/Year)

Children's Names/Ages

(First	Middle	Last	Age)
(First	Middle	Last	Age)
(First	Middle	Last	Age)
(First	Middle	Last	Age)

Career

_____

_____

_____

Hobbies

_____

_____

_____

Favorite Colors

_____

_____

_____

Favorite Foods

_____

_____

_____

Favorite Movies

_____

_____

_____

Favorite Activities

_____

_____

_____

Favorite Sports

_____

_____

_____

Parents' Names

_____
(Father)
_____
(Mother)
_____
(Stepfather or Guardian)
_____
(Stepmother or Guardian)

Siblings

_____

_____

_____

_____

Sex and Love

_____

_____

_____

_____

_____

_____

Baggage

_____

_____

_____

_____

_____

_____

What kind of relationship does this person want?

_____

_____

_____

_____

_____

_____

_____

_____

_____

_____

_____

_____

_____

_____

_____

_____

Insert a favorite photo of this person in the space below.

What makes this photo special?

_____

_____

_____

Relationship #5 Ten Points Checklist

1. Characteristics/Personality

_____

_____

_____

_____

_____

(Score)

2. Loyalty

_____

_____

_____

_____

_____

_____

(Score)

3. Trustworthiness

_____

_____

_____

_____

_____

_____
(Score)

4. Sense of Humor

_____

_____

_____

_____

_____

_____
(Score)

5. Things in Common

_____

_____

_____

_____

_____

_____
(Score)

6. Likes

_____

_____

_____

_____

_____

_____
(Score)

7. Dislikes

_____

_____

_____

_____

_____

_____

(Score)

8. Spirituality

_____

_____

_____

_____

_____

_____

(Score)

9. Family Values

_____

_____

_____

_____

_____

_____
(Score)

10. Goals

_____

_____

_____

_____

_____

_____
(Score)

Overall Score for Relationship #5

_____/_____
Score   Date

Overall Summary for Relationship #5

_____

_____

_____

_____

_____

_____

_____

_____

_____

_____

_____

_____

_____

Relationship #6 Basic Information

Name

_____/_____
(First   Middle   Last   / the date you met)

Address

_____
(Street)

_____
(City and State)

_____
(Zip Code)

Telephone Numbers

_____
(Home)

_____
(Cellular/Pager)

_____
(Work)

Email

_____
(Email Address)

_____
(Website)

Date of Birth

_____

(Month/Date/Year)

Children's Names/Ages

_____
(First   Middle   Last   Age)
_____
(First   Middle   Last   Age)
_____
(First   Middle   Last   Age)
_____
(First   Middle   Last   Age)

Career

_____

_____

_____

Hobbies

_____

_____

_____

Favorite Colors

_____

_____

_____

Favorite Foods

_____

_____

_____

Favorite Movies

_____

_____

_____

Favorite Activities

_____

_____

_____

Favorite Sports

_____

_____

_____

Parents' Names

_____
(Father)

_____
(Mother)

_____
(Stepfather or Guardian)

_____
(Stepmother or Guardian)

Siblings

_____

_____

_____

_____

_____

Sex and Love

_____

_____

_____

_____

_____

_____

Baggage

_____

_____

_____

_____

_____

_____

What kind of relationship does this person want?

_____

_____

_____

_____

_____

_____

_____

_____

_____

_____

_____

_____

_____

Insert a favorite photo of this person in the space below.

What makes this photo special?

_____

_____

_____

Relationship #6 Ten Points Checklist

1. Characteristics/Personality

_____

_____

_____

_____

_____

_____

(Score)

2. Loyalty

_____

_____

_____

_____

_____

_____

(Score)

3. Trustworthiness

_____

_____

_____

_____

_____

_____
(Score)

4. Sense of Humor

_____

_____

_____

_____

_____

_____
(Score)

5. Things in Common

_____

_____

_____

_____

_____

_____
(Score)

6. Likes

_____

_____

_____

_____

_____

_____
(Score)

7. Dislikes

_____

_____

_____

_____

_____

_____
(Score)

8. Spirituality

_____

_____

_____

_____

_____

_____
(Score)

9. Family Values

_____

_____

_____

_____

_____

_____
(Score)

10. Goals

_____

_____

_____

_____

_____

_____
(Score)

Overall Score for Relationship #6

_____/_____
Score   Date

Overall Summary for Relationship #6

_____

_____

_____

_____

_____

_____

_____

_____

_____

_____

_____

_____

Relationship #7 Basic Information

Name

_____ / _____
(First   Middle   Last   / the date you met)

Address

_____
(Street)

_____
(City and State)

_____
(Zip Code)

Telephone Numbers

_____
(Home)

_____
(Cellular/Pager)

_____
(Work)

Email

_____
(Email Address)

_____
(Website)

Date of Birth

_____

(Month/Date/Year)

Children's Names/Ages

(First	Middle	Last	Age)
(First	Middle	Last	Age)
(First	Middle	Last	Age)
(First	Middle	Last	Age)

Career

_____

_____

_____

Hobbies

_____

_____

_____

Favorite Colors

_____

_____

_____

Favorite Foods

_____

_____

_____

Favorite Movies

_____

_____

_____

Favorite Activities

_____

_____

_____

Favorite Sports

_____

_____

_____

Parents' Names

_____
(Father)

_____
(Mother)

_____
(Stepfather or Guardian)

_____
(Stepmother or Guardian)

Siblings

_____

_____

_____

_____

_____

Sex and Love

_____

_____

_____

_____

_____

_____

Baggage

_____

_____

_____

_____

_____

_____

What kind of relationship does this person want?

_____

_____

_____

_____

_____

_____

_____

_____

_____

_____

_____

_____

_____

_____

Insert a favorite photo of this person in the space below.

What makes this photo special?

_____

_____

_____

Relationship #7 Ten Points Checklist

1. Characteristics/Personality

_____

_____

_____

_____

_____

_____
(Score)

2. Loyalty

_____

_____

_____

_____

_____

_____
(Score)

3. Trustworthiness

_____

_____

_____

_____

_____

_____
(Score)

4. Sense of Humor

_____

_____

_____

_____

_____

_____
(Score)

5. Things in Common

_____

_____

_____

_____

_____

_____
(Score)

6. Likes

_____

_____

_____

_____

_____

_____
(Score)

7. Dislikes

_____

_____

_____

_____

_____

_____
(Score)

8. Spirituality

_____

_____

_____

_____

_____

_____
(Score)

9. Family Values

_____

_____

_____

_____

_____

_____
(Score)

10. Goals

_____

_____

_____

_____

_____

_____
(Score)

Overall Score for Relationship #7

_____/_____
  Score   Date

Overall Summary for Relationship #7

_____

_____

_____

_____

_____

_____

_____

_____

_____

_____

_____

_____

_____

_____

Relationship #8 Basic Information

Name

_____/_____
(First   Middle   Last   / the date you met)

Address

_____
(Street)

_____
(City and State)

_____
(Zip Code)

Telephone Numbers

_____
(Home)

_____
(Cellular/Pager)

_____
(Work)

Email

_____
(Email Address)

_____
(Website)

Date of Birth

_____

(Month/Date/Year)

Children's Names/Ages

_____
(First   Middle   Last   Age)
_____
(First   Middle   Last   Age)
_____
(First   Middle   Last   Age)
_____
(First   Middle   Last   Age)

Career

_____

_____

_____

Hobbies

_____

_____

_____

Favorite Colors

_____

_____

_____

Favorite Foods

_____

_____

_____

Favorite Movies

_____

_____

_____

Favorite Activities

_____

_____

_____

Favorite Sports

_____

_____

_____

Parents' Names

_____
(Father)

_____
(Mother)

_____
(Stepfather or Guardian)

_____
(Stepmother or Guardian)

Siblings

_____

_____

_____

_____

Sex and Love

_____

_____

_____

_____

_____

_____

Baggage

_____

_____

_____

_____

_____

What kind of relationship does this person want?

_____

_____

_____

_____

_____

_____

_____

_____

_____

_____

_____

_____

_____

_____

Insert a favorite photo of this person in the space below.

What makes this photo special?

_____

_____

_____

Relationship #8 Ten Points Checklist

1. Characteristics/Personality

_____

_____

_____

_____

_____

_____
(Score)

2. Loyalty

_____

_____

_____

_____

_____

_____
(Score)

3. Trustworthiness

_____

_____

_____

_____

_____

_____
(Score)

4. Sense of Humor

_____

_____

_____

_____

_____

_____
(Score)

5. Things in Common

_____

_____

_____

_____

_____

_____
(Score)

6. Likes

_____

_____

_____

_____

_____

_____
(Score)

7. Dislikes

_____

_____

_____

_____

_____

_____
(Score)

8. Spirituality

_____

_____

_____

_____

_____

_____
(Score)

9. Family Values

_____

_____

_____

_____

_____

_____
(Score)

10. Goals

_____

_____

_____

_____

_____

_____
(Score)

Overall Score for Relationship #8

_____/_____
   Score   Date

Overall Summary for Relationship #8

_____

_____

_____

_____

_____

_____

_____

_____

_____

_____

_____

_____

Relationship #9 Basic Information

Name

_____/_____
(First   Middle   Last   / the date you met)

Address

_____
(Street)

_____
(City and State)

_____
(Zip Code)

Telephone Numbers

_____
(Home)

_____
(Cellular/Pager)

_____
(Work)

Email

_____
(Email Address)

_____
(Website)

Date of Birth

_____

(Month/Date/Year)

Children's Names/Ages

(First	Middle	Last	Age)
(First	Middle	Last	Age)
(First	Middle	Last	Age)
(First	Middle	Last	Age)

Career

_____

_____

_____

Hobbies

_____

_____

_____

Favorite Colors

_____

_____

_____

Favorite Foods

_____

_____

_____

Favorite Movies

_____

_____

_____

Favorite Activities

_____

_____

_____

Favorite Sports

_____

_____

_____

Parents' Names

_____
(Father)

_____
(Mother)

_____
(Stepfather or Guardian)

_____
(Stepmother or Guardian)

Siblings

_____

_____

_____

_____

_____

Sex and Love

_____

_____

_____

_____

_____

Baggage

_____

_____

_____

_____

_____

What kind of relationship does this person want?

_____

_____

_____

_____

_____

_____

_____

_____

_____

_____

_____

_____

_____

_____

Insert a favorite photo of this person in the space below.

What makes this photo special?

_____

_____

_____

Relationship #9 Ten Points Checklist

1. Characteristics/Personality

_____

_____

_____

_____

_____

_____
(Score)

2. Loyalty

_____

_____

_____

_____

_____

_____
(Score)

3. Trustworthiness

_____

_____

_____

_____

_____

_____
(Score)

4. Sense of Humor

_____

_____

_____

_____

_____

_____
(Score)

5. Things in Common

_____

_____

_____

_____

_____

_____

(Score)

6. Likes

_____

_____

_____

_____

_____

_____

(Score)

7. Dislikes

_____

_____

_____

_____

_____

_____
(Score)

8. Spirituality

_____

_____

_____

_____

_____

_____
(Score)

9. Family Values

_____

_____

_____

_____

_____

_____

(Score)

10. Goals

_____

_____

_____

_____

_____

_____

(Score)

Overall Score for Relationship #9

_____/_____
Score   Date

Overall Summary for Relationship #9

_____

_____

_____

_____

_____

_____

_____

_____

_____

_____

_____

_____

_____

_____

Relationship #10 Basic Information

Name

_____/_____
(First   Middle   Last   / the date you met)

Address

_____
(Street)

_____
(City and State)

_____
(Zip Code)

Telephone Numbers

_____
(Home)

_____
(Cellular/Pager)

_____
(Work)

Email

_____
(Email Address)

_____
(Website)

Date of Birth

_____

(Month/Date/Year)

Children's Names/Ages

_____

(First   Middle   Last   Age)

_____

(First   Middle   Last   Age)

_____

(First   Middle   Last   Age)

_____

(First   Middle   Last   Age)

Career

_____

_____

_____

Hobbies

_____

_____

_____

Favorite Colors

_____

_____

_____

Favorite Foods

_____

_____

_____

Favorite Movies

_____

_____

_____

Favorite Activities

_____

_____

_____

Favorite Sports

_____

_____

_____

Parents' Names

_____
(Father)

_____
(Mother)

_____
(Stepfather or Guardian)

_____
(Stepmother or Guardian)

Siblings

_____

_____

_____

_____

_____

Sex and Love

_____

_____

_____

_____

_____

_____

Baggage

_____

_____

_____

_____

_____

_____

What kind of relationship does this person want?

Insert a favorite photo of this person in the space below.

What makes this photo special?

_____

_____

_____

Relationship #10 Ten Points Checklist

1. Characteristics/Personality

_____

_____

_____

_____

_____

_____
(Score)

2. Loyalty

_____

_____

_____

_____

_____

_____
(Score)

3. Trustworthiness

_____

_____

_____

_____

_____

_____
(Score)

4. Sense of Humor

_____

_____

_____

_____

_____

_____
(Score)

5. Things in Common

_____

_____

_____

_____

_____

_____
(Score)

6. Likes

_____

_____

_____

_____

_____

_____
(Score)

7. Dislikes

_____

_____

_____

_____

_____

_____
(Score)

8. Spirituality

_____

_____

_____

_____

_____

_____
(Score)

9. Family Values

_____

_____

_____

_____

_____
(Score)

10. Goals

_____

_____

_____

_____

_____
(Score)

Overall Score for Relationship #10

_____/_____
Score   Date

Overall Summary for Relationship #10

_____

_____

_____

_____

_____

_____

_____

_____

_____

_____

About the Author

Mary B. Morrison is the national best-selling author of her debut novel *Soul Mates Dissipate* and the author of a book of forty-six thought provoking poems entitled *Justice Just Us Just Me*.

After working eighteen years for the government, Mary quit her job on June 3, 2000, and never looked back. Earning a GS-14 salary of seventy-five thousand dollars a year from the United States Department of Housing and Urban Development was no incentive for this risk-taker to continue working nine-to-five.

Mary was born in Aurora, Illinois, reared in New Orleans, Louisiana, lived in Oakland, California for twelve years and currently resides in the Washington, D.C. Metropolitan Area. Throughout Mary's travels, she's acquired wisdom about life, love, and relationships. Mary has taken the time to share with you some of her insightful strategies for finding an ideal mate.

She is President and Founder of Booga Bear Publishing, a self-publishing company established in 1999 for the purpose of promoting her works and sharing self-publishing information with aspiring writers.

Mary is an author, poet, and lecturer. To schedule signings and/or public speaking engagements, contact Mary's publicist, Felicia Polk, at FeliciasPR@aol.com or logon to www.marymorrison.com.